Walks in
James Herriot Country

by

Malcolm Boyes

Dalesman Books
1989

The Dalesman Publishing Company Ltd.,
Clapham, Lancaster, LA2 8EB.
First published 1985
Second edition 1989
© Malcolm Boyes 1985, 1989
ISBN: 0 85206 964 2

Dedication: To Mum — Olive Chester

Printed by Swannack Brown & Co. Ltd., Hull.

Contents

Acknowledgements: The author would like to thank Hazel Chester for the maps and drawings and for her assistance in the preparation of this book.

Introduction

THE pastoral area between the Yorkshire Dales and the North York Moors has become familiar to millions of people through the books of James Herriot. The leafy lanes; the barns and stone walls of Wensleydale and Swaledale; the heather-clad moors on the western edge of the North York Moors and the streams and rivers that flow through the Vale of York have appeared as the backcloth to the films and T.V. series about a vet's life.

This book is written to take the walker and tourist into the fields and lanes, across the moors and to some of the other interesting places in the area. For centuries parties of raiding Scots used this area as a route south. Walks in the book visit the castles at Middleham and Richmond and the abbeys at Easby and Jervaulx. Later, peaceful Scottish drovers brought their cattle south along the Hambleton Drove Road to the English markets; today it offers a fine walk in two of the routes in this book. To the south of the area are Brimham Rocks — sculptured into fantastic shapes by wind erosion, the quaint and interesting town of Knaresborough, and Harrogate, one of the most popular touring bases for this area.

The walks also visit places associated with the T.V. series *All Creatures Great and Small* — Askrigg, which was the setting for Skeldale House; Langthwaite and Reeth, both of which appeared in the series a number of times; and Wensley Church where James Herriot's wedding was filmed. There is also a walk from Thirsk on which the fictional town of Darrowby is based.

All the walks are circular and start from a town or village, or a place where parking is available. Please don't obstruct other traffic or block farm gateways — you may stop a vet carrying out his important work.

Route Finding

With the aid of this book finding the route should be relatively easy. With modern farming methods hedges and walls can disappear, a path may be ploughed up to be replaced later, extra buildings may appear around a farm or old ones disappear, temporary wire fences may be placed across a field while animals graze but all routes are walkable at the time of writing. Any problems with paths or stiles should be reported to the North Yorkshire County Highways Department, County Hall, Northallerton, North Yorkshire.

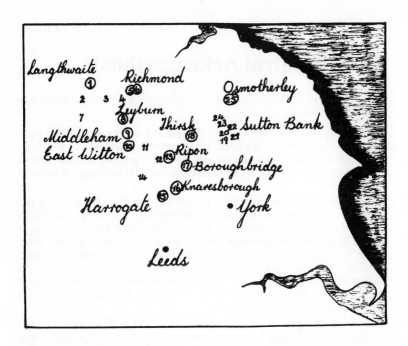

Equipment

Lightweight boots or strong walking shoes are practically a 'must', even in summer some of the paths near farms can be muddy. You also need a windproof jacket. Other pieces of equipment you may wish to carry are a compass, a whistle and waterproofs. If you are setting out in the evening or may be finishing in the dark a torch should be carried. Ordnance Survey maps to cover the walks are Sheet 92 for walks 1 – 6 (part of walk 3 is on Sheet 99). Sheet 104 covers walks 15 and 16. Walks 19 to 24 are covered by Sheet 100. Walk 25 is on three maps — Sheets 93, 99 and 100 or on the North York Moors tourist map. The rest of the walks appear on Sheet 99.

5

Central Arkengarthdale

Start: NZ004024. The entrance to Langthwaite village from the Reeth to Tan Hill Inn road.

FROM the point where the road turns into Langthwaite village walk over the bridge which featured in the opening sequence of the T.V. series *All Creatures Great and Small.* Turn left just beyond the shop in the village, pass through a gate, and cross the field keeping a stone wall on your left.

Pass through a gate beside a ruined barn and continue along the wallside. Pass through a stile and follow the wire fence skirting a depression, continue through a gateway and head towards the large house. A gate below the house gives access to a drive which leads into a road. Turn right along the road and after twenty yards turn left, before a bend in the road, on a track above the river. The path climbs over a footbridge to a gate. Continue walking alongside the wire fence above the river. Pass through a stile and cross the field, climbing over a stile on the left of a gate to reach the road.

Turn left along the road and cross over the bridge. Turn right through a stile near a gate and follow the path to a footbridge. Cross over the bridge and turn left to a squeeze stile set in the wall (yellow arrow); the path continues along the river bank.

Pass over a footbridge near Wood House and continue through stiles and gateways towards Whaw. As you approach Whaw pass through a gateway beside a barn, then pass through a gateway beside a modern barn to reach the road where you turn left. Pass over the bridge and continue to the main road. Turn left, and after passing six buildings turn left through a gate off the road. Walk down the field keeping a wall on your left, then cross the field to a gate which leads down to the river. Follow a path along the riverside, ignore the footbridge over the river and continue along the bank; eventually the path climbs above the river, then descends to a gate and small footbridge over a stream. Turn right at the end of the next field along a wallside, pass through two gates to the right of a house and follow the lane. You pass the site of the famous Octagon lead smelting mill on your right, then the road curves right to the road.

At the opposite side of the road are the ruins of the New Mill which was also used for smelting lead. Turn left down the road to the junction. In the field on your left you can see the hexagonal powder house standing alone — it was used to store explosives for the mines.

Turn left at the junction onto the Bowes Road. Turn right near a wall letter box, pass through a gate and walk along the track. Turn left at a

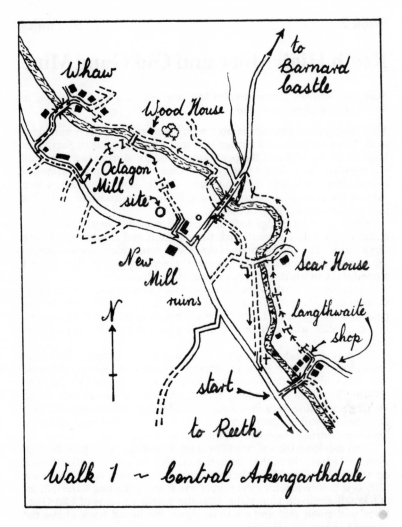

Walk 1 ~ Central Arkengarthdale

junction, between walls, then turn right just before a bridge along a tarmac road to Langthwaite church. Turn left down the road and turn left again back over the bridge into Langthwaite village.

Reeth High Moor and Old Gang Mine

Start: SD 988999. Surrender Bridge, one mile north of Feetham, in Swaledale, on the road to Langthwaite.

THIS walk passes through an area wich has been extensively mined for lead. Close to Surrender Bridge (see map) are the ruins of Surrender Lead Smelting Mill and the peat house used for storing fuel. The mill was powered by a 22 foot waterwheel. One of the common features of the smelting mills are the long flues, usually now collapsed, which carried the poisonous fumes up the hillside away from the mill. This lead mill ceased working in 1881.

From Surrender Bridge walk up the road towards Langthwaite. After quarter of a mile a stoned track turns off left and climbs onto Reeth High Moor. The road continues down to a ford which was featured in the opening sequence of *All Creatures Great and Small*. The distinct stoned track twists its way onto Reeth High Moor.

After one and a half miles the track passes a sheep fold on your right. Continue, heading for a stake set in a spoil heap on the skyline. As you pass through the spoil heaps the track becomes indistinct descending into the valley with a stone wall about a hundred yards away on your right.

The path descends to a gate in a stone wall and gives access to a broad track along the valley. Fork left after the stream and continue along the main track in the valley bottom to reach the ruins of Level House. The building was used as a lodging house, possibly by miners who would spend the working week in this remote valley rather than make the long daily return walk to their homes in Swaledale and Arkengarthdale, a thankless journey, especially in the depths of winter.

Continue down the valley and bear left at a bridge, then pass through a gate but ignore the path rising to the left after the gravel works. As you approach Old Gang Mines the peat store on the hillside comes into view first. Just before reaching the ruins there is an interesting waterfall, set in a small gorge on your right. Pass the extensive ruins of Old Gang Mine and smelt mill and continue down the broad track above the stream to Surrender Bridge.

The Old Gang Mine closed about 1885; the smelting mill was built about 1790. It was powered by a 24 foot diameter waterwheel which worked the air pumps for the four furnaces. A long flue ran across the moor to a chimney on Healaugh Crag. The vast peat house on the hillside was some 387 feet long and housed a year's supply of peat for the mill; the stone piers carried a thatched roof and the open sides allowed the wind to dry the peat.

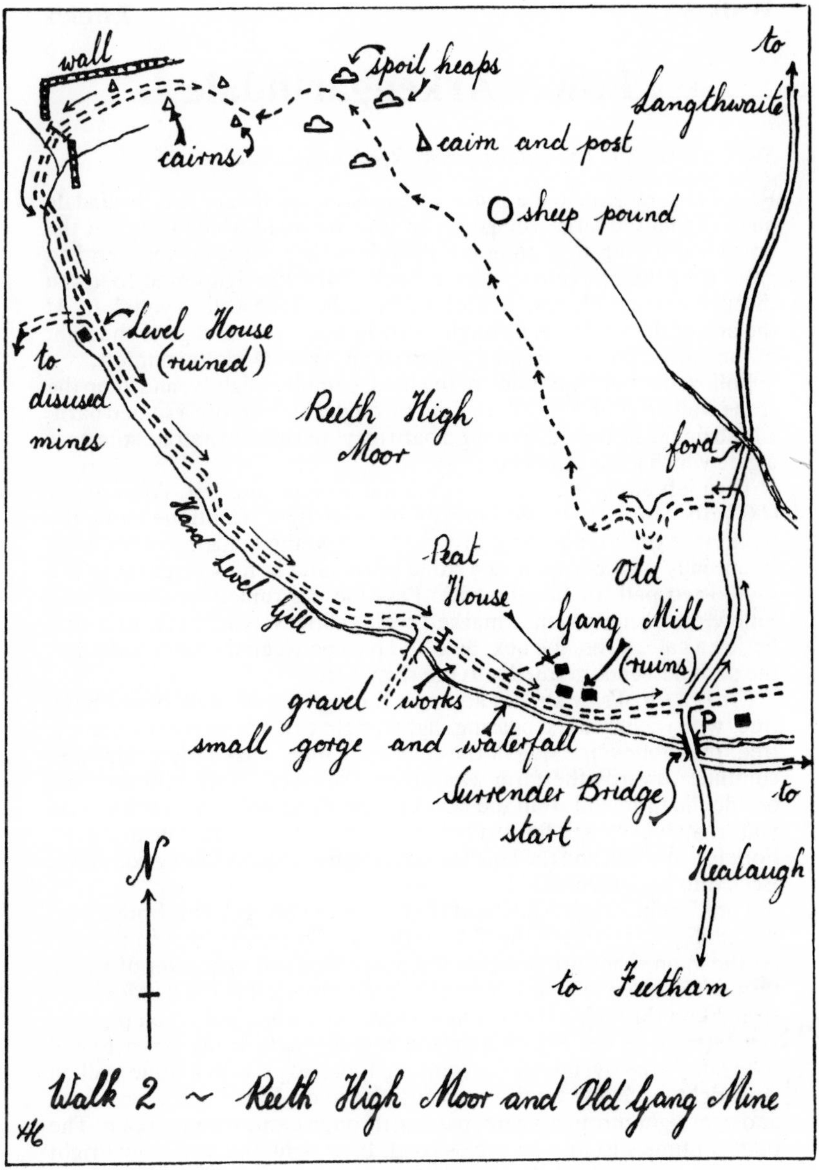

wall

spoil heaps

cairns

cairn and post

O sheep pound

to Langthwaite

Level House
(ruined)

to
disused
mines

Reeth High
Moor

ford

Hard Level Gill

Peat
House

Old
Gang Mill
(ruins)

gravel works

small gorge and waterfall

Surrender Bridge
start

P

to
Healaugh

to Feetham

N

Walk 2 ~ Reeth High Moor and Old Gang Mine

46

9

Lower Arkengarthdale

Start: SE038993. The village green, Reeth in Swaledale.

REETH stands near the point where Arkengarthdale and Swaledale meet. From the large village green take the road which leaves at the bottom and leads to Richmond. Pass the police house on your left and cross over the bridge over Arkle Beck. Take the signposted footpath through a stone stile and turn left keeping the stone wall on your left. At the end of the field pass through a stile beside a gate and go to the right of the barns. There is a small waterfall on Arkle Beck to your left.

Follow the right hand side of the field, climbing slightly, and keep the stone wall on your right. Turn right through a stile before a ruined barn. Climb up the next field, passing a barn on your right, to a stone stile near a gate which leads into a lane.

Turn left along the track keeping the wall on your left. After about 600 yards you pass an old limekiln on your right. Continue along the track, with the stream about fifty yards below; this leads into woodland. Eventually pass between two stone pillars and in fifty yards there is a signposted path to Langthwaite. Pass the old ruined farmhouse and follow the rising ground, marked with yellow waymarkers, to a stile beside a gate. Cross the next field and pass between the farm buildings; the path descends gradually to the riverside.

Cross a small side stream and pass through a gate, walk beneath the trees with waymarkers, bearing slightly right to a waymarker on a single tree, then follow the side of the river for a mile. Pass a footbridge and continue towards the farm away from the river. Walk into the lane beside the farm and continue between the stone walls, pass a house on your right and cross a footbridge, beside a ford, and climb up to a gate. Fork left at a sign and the lane leads through woods and alongside Arkle Beck into Langthwaite.

Turn left in Langthwaite and cross over the bridge. This bridge may be familiar to you from the T.V. series *All Creatures Great and Small*. At the main road turn left past the post office and in quarter of a mile turn left into Arkle Town. When the road turns left in the hamlet carry straight on through a stile, beside a gate, in a stone wall. You pass the gravestones in the old churchyard and the path leads down to the riverside; cross over a stile beyond the footbridge, with a stone wall on your right — yellow arrows waymark the stiles. Eventually pass a farm and bear right through a gate, passing through a stile over a stream. The path continues to join an access road, bear right and at the next right turn carry straight on. A series of stiles in the walls leads to the road to the right of Sleights Brow House where you can turn left down the road into Reeth.

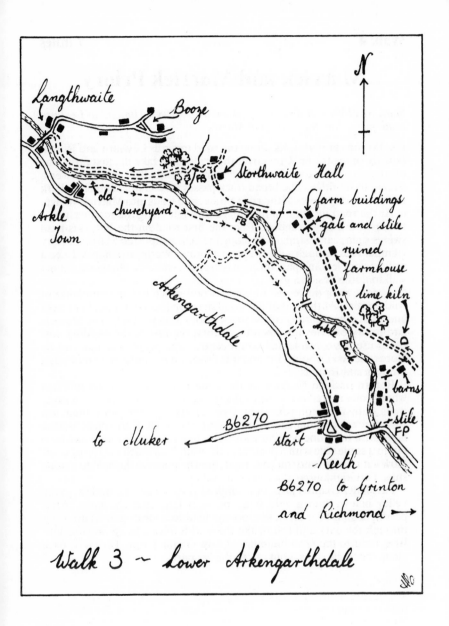

N

Langthwaite

Booze

Storthwaite Hall

farm buildings

gate and stile

old churchyard

Arkle Town

FB

FB

ruined farmhouse

lime kiln

Arkengarthdale

Arkle Beck

D

barns

stile FP

B6270

start

to Muker

Reeth

B6270 to Grinton and Richmond

Walk 3 ~ Lower Arkengarthdale

Walk 4   7 miles

Marrick and Marrick Priory

Start: SE115994. A large car park on the A6108 Richmond to Leyburn road, just before the turn off to Marske.

FROM the car park walk along the road towards Leyburn and Reeth. Beware of the traffic. Cross over the bridge and take the first farm lane on the left, just above the river bank. Eventually you cross over a stream by a bridge. The broad track passes Low Oxque and High Park farms, offering views of the river Swale, and leads into Marrick village.

At the road junction in the village turn left along the road passing a house with a large sundial. Take the first road on the left; this road swings right, carry straight on along the lane signposted Marrick Priory ¾ mile. Pass through a gate beyond a former Wesleyan Chapel. Keep a wall on your left and pass through two gates; continue alongside a stone wall to a stile beside a gate.

A stone path descends through a wood which has an abundance of wild flowers. At the end of the wood the path joins the road; bear right and cross over a cattle grid. Marrick Priory is on your left. The grounds and priory exterior are open to visitors, the rest of the building now being used as a residential youth centre. The priory was founded by Robert de Aske about 1165 and was dissolved in 1540 when there was a prioress and 16 nuns.

Return back to Marrick by the same route. At the road junction where you entered the village take the signposted lane, between stone walls, with a farm on your right. Bear left through two gates, then turn right through another gate, with a barn on your left. Carry on across the field, with the stone wall on your right, to a gate, pass a barn and bear left to a stone stile with a post set in the wall. You reach the top of Croft How with a wire fence on your right, then bear across the field to a stone stile. Turn right along the top of the valley.

Pass High Oxque Farm, one hundred yards away on your left, in the valley below. Join a wire fence on your left, after the farm. After passing a gate bear left and cross the field to a lower gate. Turn right through the gate and follow the track with a wire fence on your left. Bear right to the farm buildings at Low Oxque Farm. Turn left, back along the track you set out on, to the car park.

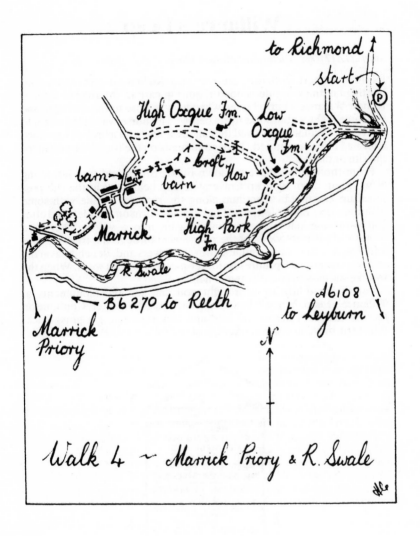

to Richmond

start

High Oxque Fm.   Low Oxque Fm.

barn →   croft How

barn   How

Marrick   High Park Fm.

R. Swale

B6270 to Reeth

A6108 to Leyburn

Marrick Priory

N

Walk 4 ~ Marrick Priory & R. Swale

Willance's Leap

Start: NZ171008. Richmond Market Place.

IN 1606 Robert Willance, the son of a Richmond grocer, was out hunting. A thick fog descended requiring care in the rugged terrain. Robert Willance's horse bolted when he was close to the cliff edge and fell some 200 feet onto the rocks below. The horse was killed outright but Robert Willance survived the fall, escaping with a broken leg which later had to be amputated. Two monuments on the top of the cliff mark the site of the fall.

From the Market Place go down Finkle Street and turn left along Newbiggen. Turn right up Cravengate and bear right at the sub post office up Westfields. Continue along the road for a mile with some pleasant views on the left, pass High Leases Farm on your left and after 200 yards the path goes through a gate into a wood. There are occasional pleasant views of the river Swale through the trees on your left. The wood contains a number of wild flowers and, depending on the season, you may see primroses, forget-me-nots or wild roses. When the wood ends pass over a stile into a field.

On the crag top to your right you can see the monuments at Willance's Leap. You will be walking back past them later. Continue on the distinct track across the field and fork right along a grass track, indicated by yellow waymarkers, just before a farm. Pass over a stile.

14

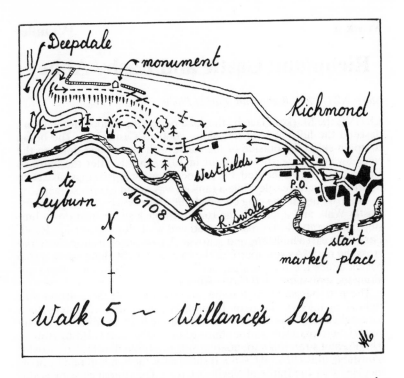

Walk 5 ~ Willance's Leap

Keep the next farm buildings on your left and continue to a gate at the end of the field which leads to a tarmac road.

Cross the road and keep the stone wall on your left, then head for a stile in a stone wall. Cross the stile and continue over the field to a stile near a gate which leads to a tarmac road. Turn right up the road, turn left at the junction and cross over a cattle grid; the tarmac road then swings right into Deepdale.

Continue up the valley and twenty yards before the cattle grid, at the head of the dale, turn back sharp right along the top of the valley, following the wall along the cliff top. There are some fine views, firstly into Deepdale and later across the fields and woods into Swaledale. The path swings left and heads for Willance's Leap. From the two monuments on the site of the fall you can look over the cliff to the path you walked along earlier.

Continue along the cliff top passing over two stiles and then walk straight on along the edge of a field to pass some gorse bushes and reach a gate. At this point there is a fine view over the Vale of York to the Cleveland Hills. Pass through the gate and follow the track which curves right to High Leases Farm. Turn back left down the road back into Richmond.

15

Richmond Castle and Easby Abbey

Start: NZ171008. Richmond Market Place.

LEAVE the Market Place by the road beside the Talbot Hotel. Don't descend the hill but bear left along cobbled Castle Hill. The broad footpath skirts the outside of the castle with good views down to the river Swale. The castle was built in 1071, shortly after the Norman Conquest, by Alan the Red. On two occasions Scottish kings have been imprisoned in the castle while a ransom was raised to release them.

You pass beside the crag on which the castle was built. As you leave Castle Walk and approach the road turn back sharp right down four steps; in twenty yards cross the road and walk down Riverside Road. Fork right past a millstone and gearwheel, pass through an archway and cross the park. As you approach the road turn right along a path which passes under the road bridge, beside the river. Turn left, then right along the lane signposted Easby Abbey.

The path passes through some fine woodland; at the junction fork right along the riverside path. Eventually you climb a set of steps, then turn right over a stile. Follow the edge of the field, keeping a hedge on your right, cross a stile and continue round to the ruins of Easby Abbey. The Premonstratensian foundation was established in 1152 by Roald, Constable of Richmond Castle. It suffered at the hands of raiding Scots in 1346, after the Battle of Neville's Cross. The church close by is also interesting and contains wall paintings and a replica of the 7th or 8th century Easby Cross.

After passing the church bear left along the road. You pass the abbey gatehouse in the field on your right. Take the first lane on your left — this offers views of the church and abbey — and after 120 yards turn left over a stile in a wooden fence. Follow the track to the next field which descends beneath the trees to a stile. Cross the next field to the start of a stone wall, cross over the stile and carry straight on with a wall on your right.

Continue walking along the path where you forked off earlier. The lane turns left to the main road above the bridge. Turn right up the road, passing the interesting church on your right; at the top, turn left, back into the bottom of the Market Place.

In Ryders Wynd, the road to the right just before you reach the Market Place, is the Richmondshire Museum offering a glance of life in old Richmond.

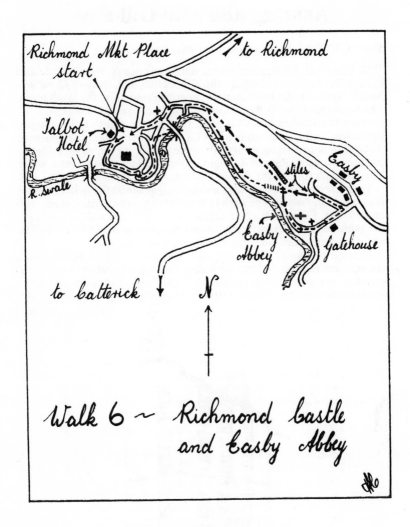

Walk 6 ~ Richmond Castle and Easby Abbey

Askrigg and Mill Gill Foss

Start: SD947910. From the market cross near the church.

THE village of Askrigg lies on the northern edge of Wensleydale and became the familiar setting for the T.V. series *All Creatures Great and Small.* Opposite the market cross, near the church, is the large house which became familiar to millions of people as Skeldale House.

From the market cross take the road to the right of the church, signposted as the footpath to Mill Gill Foss. As you leave the houses of Askrigg behind turn right through a stile, beside a gate, along a flagged path over a field. Pass to the right of the buildings and under a water leat; the path follows the side of a stream.

Turn left over the footbridge and bear right across the field back into the edge of the wood. The path climbs above the river with a stone wall on your left. Eventually you reach a stone stile in the wall on your left; the path descends to the right, dropping down to Mill Gill Foss. The waterfall drops some seventy feet over a limestone lip.

Retrace your steps back to the stone stile set in the wall, pass through the stile and turn right along the wallside up a grassy hollow way. There is a fine view across Wensleydale to Bainbridge. Turn right through a stile just beyond the barn and follow the wall on your right to a stile.

Askrigg's "Skeldale House"

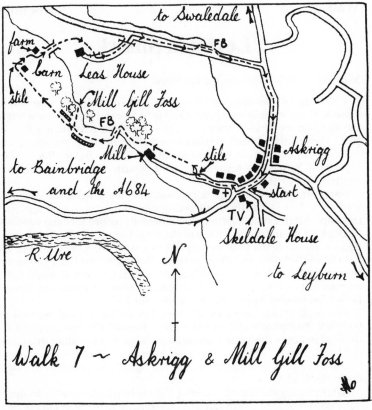

Walk 7 ~ Askrigg & Mill Gill Foss

Fifteen yards from the farm turn right through a gate, cross a field, keeping the stone wall on your left, to a stile and the path continues over a footbridge across the stream.

Carry straight on to a fingerpost stating 'To Low Straits'. Turn right at the wall corner to a gate which leads into a farm access road. Continue up the road — there is a fine panorama on the right over Wensleydale to the flat-topped hill of Addleborough on the skyline. The farm road climbs up to a gate, pass through the gate and turn right along the walled lane. The area around is the familiar Dales scenery of stone walls and green fields, many of which have their own small stone barns.

At the ford cross over the footbridge and continue to the Askrigg-Swaledale road. Turn right back down the road into Askrigg. As you approach the village you can look over the stone-tiled roofs to Addleborough. At the road junction turn right, back through the village to the cobbled square with its village pump, stone cross and Skeldale House.

Walk 8

Leyburn Shawl

Start: SE112905. Leyburn Market Place.

AT the top of the square in Leyburn, where the road turns left to Hawes, carry straight on up the road into Shawl Terrace. Turn left at the sign 'To the Shawl', then turn right through a gate along a flagged path. There are fine views, to the left, into Wensleydale; the Shawl is an outcrop of rock which runs along the daleside. By tradition Mary Queen of Scots was recaptured on Leyburn Shawl after escaping captivity in Castle Bolton.

Carry straight on through a gateway keeping a wood on your left. Pass over two stiles, the path continuing along the top of the rock outcrop. After a mile a path bears downhill; ignore this and continue through a gate and along the top of the crag, keeping a stone wall on the right. Eventually the path sweeps left to a stile; cross the corner of the field to another stile and then cross the undulating field to a gate in the bottom right hand corner. Continue over the next field with a wire fence on your left. At the end of the field turn left through a gate and along a farm road passing Tullis Cote Farm on your left.

The road sweeps down to the Wensley-Redmire road, passing on your left the remains of a building which housed a pumping engine for the lead mines in this area. Pass through the gate at the other side of the road and cross the field to a stile beside the gate. Cross over the railway line and the next field to the gate in the right hand corner. Turn right down the road.

After passing the cottage on your right turn left, at a public footpath sign, down the lane. Turn left at the T-junction; the lane curves right between the farm buildings. Turn left after the gate along a broad concrete road with an iron fence on your left. Pass below Bolton Hall, on your left, and continue along the road.

After passing a lodge on your right the road eventually goes between two stone pillars and into Wensley village. To the right is Wensley Church which was used as the setting for the marriage of James Herriot in *All Creatures Great and Small*. As you pass through the two stone pillars the road to the left leads back into Leyburn.

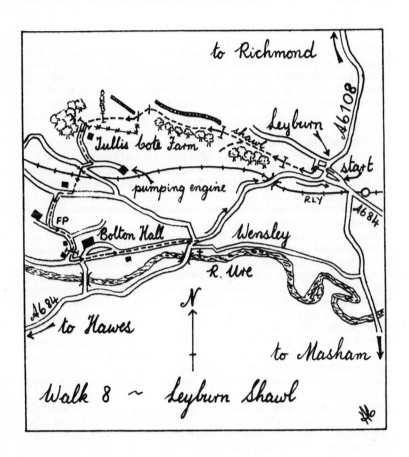

to Richmond

Leyburn

A6108

Tullis bote Farm

shawl

start

pumping engine

RLY

A684

FP

Bolton Hall

Wensley

R. Ure

A684

to Hawes

N

to Masham

Walk 8 ~ Leyburn Shawl

Middleham Castle and the River Cover

Start: SE126876. The road in front of Middleham Castle.

MIDDLEHAM CASTLE was the home of the powerful Neville Family. It was visited by numerous members of both noble and royal families and became known as the 'Windsor of the North'. During the War of the Roses it was in the hands of Richard Neville, known as Warwick the Kingmaker, from his title Earl of Warwick. After his death at the Battle of Barnet in 1471 it passed into the hands of Richard III.

Take the lane to the left of Middleham Castle and turn left in ten yards along a walled lane. Cross a field to a gate and bear left along the fence to a stile. Cross the next field to a gate into a lane, turn right along the lane and continue straight on when the road sweeps right. In fifty yards pass through a gate and carry straight on across a field, keeping a stone wall on your right, to the river Cover. Turn right over a stile and follow the path along the river bank.

Eventually you pass through a gateway into a field; cross the field to a stile in the far right corner. The path continues through woodland, beside the river to a stile into a field. Bear right on an indistinct path, uphill and through a line of trees. Continue across the field to a stile in the corner on the right. Cross the next field to rejoin the path beyond a wooden fence, overlooking the river some seventy feet below.

Eventually the path descends alongside a wire fence to a stile and the river. At the bridge follow the track to the right, then turn right at the trees in fifty yards. Walk uphill, across the field, to a gate onto the road. There is a little lake nestling in a pleasant hollow on your left. Turn right, back towards Middleham, keeping the stone wall on your right, a safer route than following the road. The wall eventually joins the road at a cattle grid; walk down the road and in 30 yards turn right through a gate and continue with the wall and the road on your left to a squeeze stile. Cross the next field to another stile then follow the left hand edge of the field to a stile into a lane. Turn left again back to the road and turn right back into Middleham passing the castle on your right.

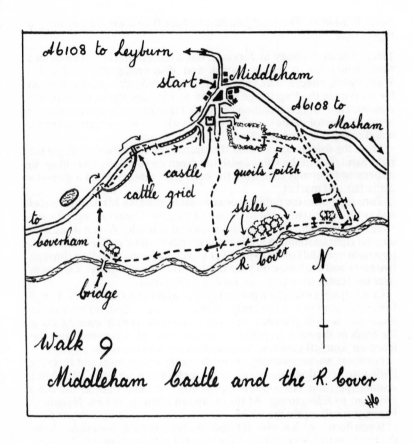

A6108 to Leyburn ←

start → Middleham

A6108 to Masham

castle

cattle grid

quoits pitch

to coverham

stiles

R. Cover

N

bridge

Walk 9
Middleham Castle and the R. Cover

The Cheese Trail

Start: SE144860. The road junction in East Witton on the Leyburn to Ripon road.

THE Cistercian abbey at Jervaulx was founded in 1147. The monks were noted for breeding horses and discovering the recipe for Wensleydale cheese. The last abbot, Adam de Sedbergh, was hanged for his part in the Pilgrimage of Grace in 1536 and the monastery was dissolved in 1537. By tradition he handed the recipe for the cheese over to the proprietor of the Cover Bridge Inn who for many years produced it and called it Coverham cheese.

From the road junction, near the church in East Witton, walk up the right hand road in the village with the green on your left. The village in its present form may date from the early 14th century when it gained a cattle fair and market.

Turn right onto the public footpath just beyond the Methodist chapel and cross the field to a stile to the left of the gate. Continue, keeping the hedge on your right, to a gate then descend to a stile. With a stone wall on your right continue to a stile in the corner of stone walls. Pass a barn, turn right over the fences to the river Cover and bear right. Pass through two gates and the hedge on your right leads to a road bridge. Turn right over the fences to steps which lead up to the road.

Cross straight over the road, unless you wish to visit the Cover Bridge Inn at the other side of the bridge. Continue beside the river with a wire fence on your left. The next one and a half miles is easy walking along the bank of the river Ure, then turn right through a gate and with the fence on your left continue one hundred yards to the road.

For those walkers wishing to visit Jervaulx Abbey ruins and Jervaulx Park turn left along the road — the entrance is on your left. After visiting the ruins continue along the road, turning right at the road junction, to Ellingstring. At the sharp left bend, near Low Newstead Farm, you will rejoin the walk.

If you do not wish to visit Jervaulx Abbey and park, turn right, down the road, an in 300 yards turn left through a gate and cross a field with a wire fence on your left. Pass through a gate and continue bearing left to a gate and stone bridge. Pass through another gate, with a wood on your left, and climb up towards the farm buildings. Curve left to a gate into a farm lane which leads to the road on your left.

Turn right and walk up the road and in half a mile turn right along the lane to Hammer Farm. Turn right behind the farmhouse to a gate. Cross the field to a gate, then cross the next field, bearing left to another gate. The track turns back sharp right to a gate into a lane. Continue down the road, forking right at the road junction into East Witton.

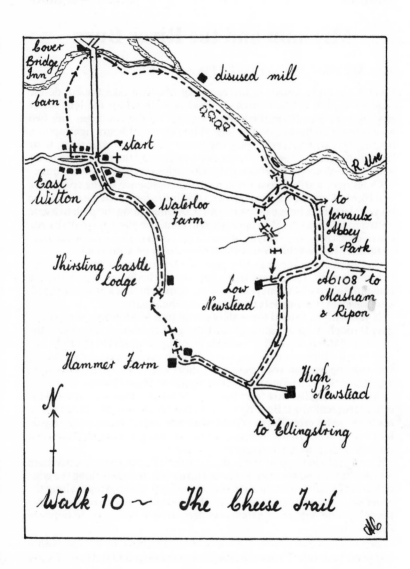

Cover Bridge Inn

barn

disused mill

start

East Wilton

R. Ure

Waterloo Farm

to Jervaulx Abbey & Park

Thirsting Castle Lodge

Low Newstead

A6108 to Masham & Ripon

Hammer Farm

High Newstead

N

to Ellingstring

Walk 10 ~ The Cheese Trail

Masham and the River Burn

Start: SE225807. Masham Market Place.

FROM the large square in the centre of Masham take the cul-de-sac road to the left of the church — there is a school on the left. After passing over a cattle grid continue straight on the road ignoring two access roads to houses on the left. When the road bears right up to a house, carry straight on keeping the house grounds on your right. Bear right through a gate and the track curves right and the river appears on your left. Follow the riverside path with fields on right for half a mile.

Cross over a stile into a wood near the confluence of the rivers Ure and Burn. A path leads through the wood into a lane with the river Burn on your left and a hedge on your right. Continue along the path to a gate onto a road, cross the stile opposite and continue along the path beside the river. Cross over a small stream on the rocks in the bed and the path eventually follows the river with a craggy bank on your right.

Continue along the path to a gate in a fence about a hundred yards before the road, then curve right, keeping the hedge on your right to a stile into the road. At this point you can turn right, back along the road, into Masham, turning left then right into the square.

If you wish to extend the walk you can turn left towards the bridge, pass through a small gate and skirt the golf clubhouse and rejoin the riverside path. Keep to the riverside ignoring the paths to the right and pass two footbridges over the river. Pass through a gate and continue with a stone wall on your right for a short while. The path bears right into a farm lane, passing through two gates to Shaws Farm.

After passing the first farm building turn right, then left, around the other farm buildings. Bear right across the field to join the hedge which leads to a gate; cross the next field, with a hedge on your right to a gate into a road. Turn right along the road to the sharp corner and turn right through a gate, along a signposted footpath.

Cross the field keeping the hedge on your left, passing a wooden barn on your left. Cross over the fence and turn right, then left along the edge of the field. Turn right through the second gate and continue along the other side of the hedge to a stile. Walk over the next field, passing under the telephone wires to a gateway. Carry straight on to a gate between two iron barns.

Bear right, then follow the track towards Masham church with a hedge on your left. Cross the field to a gate into a hedged lane. Pass a modern mill on your left and the road crosses over a small bridge; turn right along Westholme Place. The road curves right past Theakston's Brewery and at the T-junction turn left, then right, back into the

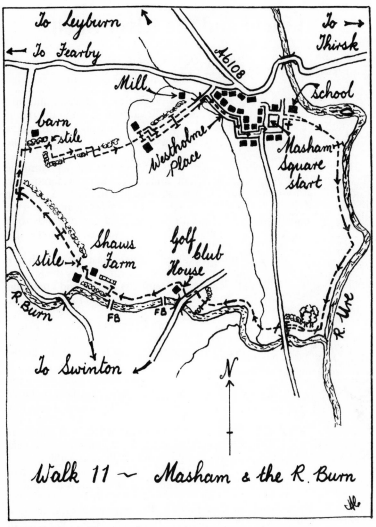

To Leyburn
To Fearby
A6108
To Thirsk
Mill
School
barn
stile
Westholme Place
Masham Square start
Shaws Farm
Golf Club House
stile
R. Burn
FB
FB
R. Ure
To Swinton
N
Walk 11 ~ Masham & the R. Burn

Market Place. There is now a visitors centre at Theakston's Brewery with a factory tour in the afternoon.

Walk 12   3¾ miles
(5 miles via Studley Park and Fountains Abbey)

Aldfield and the River Skell

Start: SE265695. The village of Aldfield, south of the Ripon to Pateley Bridge road, on the approach to Fountains Abbey.

FROM the church in the village walk down to the junction and turn right towards Fountains Abbey. After 150 yards turn left at the public footpath sign to Studley Roger. Cross the field bearing right to a stile into a lane and turn left. On approaching the obelisk turn right down the track.

If you wish to visit Studley deer park and see the church, continue through the gate in the stone wall. The church was built as a memorial to Frederick Grantham Vyner. He was captured by brigands in Greece in 1870. One of the captured party was sent with a ransom demand and the money was collected, but before it could be paid the brigands took fright, executing their prisoners. The ransom was used to build this church by his sister, the Marchioness of Ripon.

If you wish to visit Fountains Abbey continue past the church and turn sharp right after a quarter of a mile to the car park by the lake. A fee is payable and the path leads past Fountains Abbey and Fountains Hall to the road. Continue straight on to the sharp right turn where you carry straight on over the stile.

If you are not visiting the deer park and Fountains Abbey, continue down the track from the obelisk. This leads down to the road where you bear left. At the sharp bend turn right over a stile beside the public footpath sign.

Both routes now continue along the broad track which follows the wooded valley of the river Skell. After 1¼ miles you pass a ruined building on your right; turn right immediately after the ruin, it may be a little overgrown but the main path soon clears. Keep bearing right under the trees and climbing steadily to a stile where you leave the wood. Follow the hollow way curving left to a gate and cross the next field to a white gate. Turn right along the road back into Aldfield.

Fountains Abbey was established in 1132 by thirteen monks who had left St. Mary's Abbey at York. The Cistercian abbey grew into one of the richest abbeys in England; in 1539 when it was dissolved there was an abbot, a prior and thirteen monks. The extensive ruins lie in a beautiful setting beside the river Skell. Fountains Hall, completed in 1611 by Sir Stephen Proctor, was constructed with stone robbed from parts of the monastery.

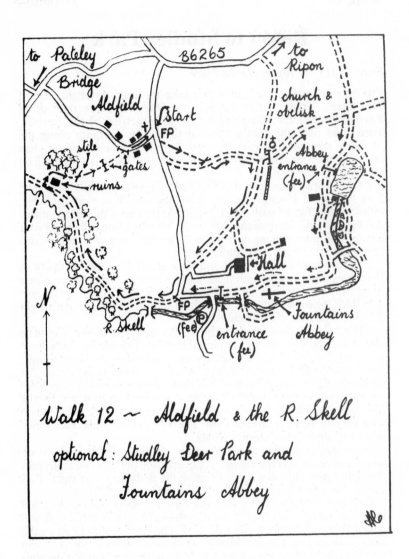

to Pateley
Bridge
Aldfield
B6265
to Ripon
church &
obelisk
Start
FP
stile
gates
ruins
Abbey
entrance
(fee)
N
Hall
FP
(fee)
entrance
(fee)
Fountains
Abbey
R. Skell

Walk 12 ~ Aldfield & the R. Skell
optional: Studley Deer Park and
Fountains Abbey

Ripon to Studley Park

Start: SE313713. Ripon Market Place.

FROM the Market Place in Ripon take the road down the side of Wakeman's House. After crossing over the river, turn right down Borrage Green Lane; this continues as a pleasant track beside the river. Turn right over the footbridge and follow the footpath along the riverside, steps leading up to the road. Turn left to the main road, then left again over the river towards Studley Roger. There is a footpath on the right side of the road.

At the Z bend take the public footpath signposted to Studley Roger. Pass through a kissing gate and keep the wire fence on your left, following the distinct path over the field. At the end of the field continue through the gate but note the path to the left which you will use on your return. Continue walking over the next two fields to a lane, behind two large trees, that leads into Studley Roger.

Cross straight over the road and walk along the public footpath to Fountains Abbey. The path leads over a field to a wooden gate in a stone wall where you enter Studley Deer Park. The path, now indistinct, bears slightly left eventually joining the road. Turn right along the road towards the church.

After 200 yards turn left along the road to the car park. You should be able to see some of the deer around this point. The avenue leads down to the lake; turn left around the edge to a footbridge. Cross the bridge, turn left and when the track forks bear left to a small stone bridge. The path turns right along the valley. The path keeps crossing the river Skell on stone bridges until you reach a gate in a stone wall. Pass through the gate and the path continues for quarter of a mile — there is a wood on your left and the river on your right. The path joins another track which bears left, uphill, into Studley Roger.

Turn right in Studley Roger along the public footpath to Ripon on which you came into the village. After crossing the first two fields pass through a gate and turn right, keeping the hedge on your right. Pass over a stile and cross two fields to a footbridge over the river.

Continue straight on to a gate and turn left along a track. Fork left after a hundred yards to join the riverside path. After half a mile you pass a Ripon Navigation pillar of 1820. The path continues along the river bank passing the footbridge you crossed earlier in the day, and into Borrage Green Lane. Turn left at the main road and retrace your steps to the Market Place.

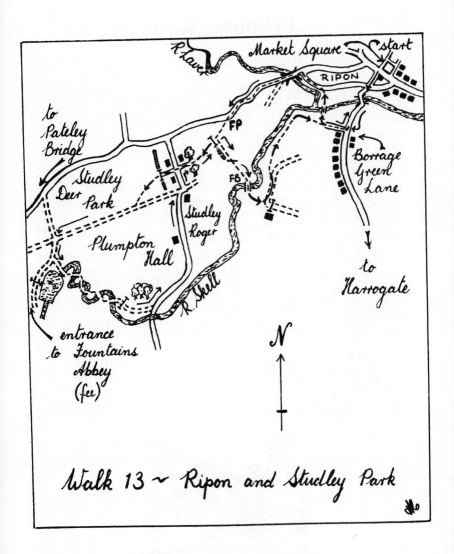

to
Pateley
Bridge

Studley
Deer
Park

Plumpton
Hall

entrance
to Fountains
Abbey
(fee)

R. Laver

Market Square

start

RIPON

FP

FB

Studley
Roger

R. Skell

Borrage
Green
Lane

to
Harrogate

N

Walk 13 ~ Ripon and Studley Park

Brimham Rocks

Start: SE208644. On the road where you turn into Brimham Rocks car park.

BRIMHAM ROCKS are a collection of weird, naturally sculptured rocks set about 1,000 feet above sea level on Brimham Moor. The route to the rocks is signposted from the Harrogate–Pateley Bridge road and from the Ripon–Pateley Bridge road. There is a National Trust car park at the site where a charge is made for parking.

From the road where you turn in to the car park take the road that forks left. After thirty yards pass through a gate; the lane heads slightly downhill with some of the rocks visible on the right. Ignore the track to the left and continue through the wood. Bear right as you approach a house, keeping a stone wall on your left. At the fork in the tracks near the barn, fork left through a gate along a stone walled lane. Fine views of Nidderdale open out in front of you.

Pass over a gate, with a stile built in, and follow the track down the field keeping a wire fence on your left. The path bears right on entering scrubland and continues round to a farmhouse. Pass over a stile beside a gate as you approach the farm, then fork right to a blue gate.

Keep the stone wall on your right and pass through the trees to a stile over a wire fence. Cross over the field to another stile then continue straight on through a belt of trees. Skirt the top side of the next field to a gate on the right. Turn right through the gate and walk up the field, with a stone wall and fence on your left, to another gate. A stile leads into a short rough lane. Bear left across the next field, climb over a stile over a wire fence, and pass below the farm buildings to a gate. Turn right along the wallside to another gate. Turn right, then left, up the field keeping the wall on your left to join the farm access road. Turn left through a

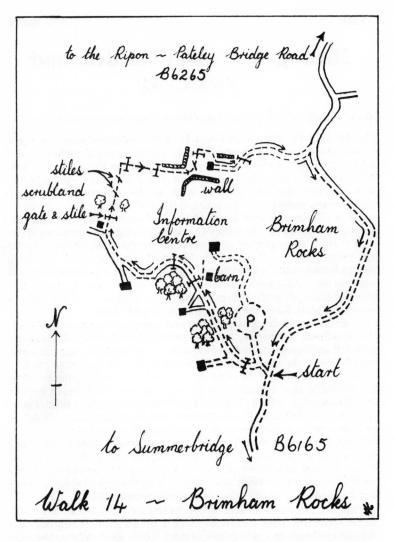

to the Ripon ~ Pateley Bridge Road
B6265

stiles
scrubland
gate & stile

wall

Information
Centre

Brimham
Rocks

barn

N

P

start

to Summerbridge   B6165

Walk 14 ~ Brimham Rocks

gate along the access road to join the main road around Brimham
Rocks. There are a number of paths which lead through the complex of
rocks to the car park. Overlooking the crags from the highest point is an
information centre. Turn right at the junction with the road along the
tarmac road across Brimham Moor. Brimham Rocks are on your right
and after a while you reach the entrance to the car park from where you
set out.

33

Harrogate's Valley Gardens and Birk Crag

Start: SE298554. The Royal Pump Room Museum, Harrogate.

HARROGATE was one of James Herriot's favourite places to take a break from his work. The large stone houses seem to cluster around the edges of the massive Stray and town's gardens. The Royal Pump Room Museum contains a collection of items on local history — the building was originally the Old Sulphur Well. In this spa town some forty different spa waters could be taken in the 19th century.

From the Royal Pump Room Museum cross over the road and pass through the gateway into Valley Gardens. Through most seasons of the year there is a fine display of flowers and shrubs. Take the path to the left which has a small stream on the left. Turn right at the children's swings between the tennis courts. Turn left where the paths cross and walk up the tarmac path with a stone wall on your right. At the start of the woodland, near the war memorial on your right, fork right onto a woodland path. Keep the war memorial on your right.

After 250 yards cross over a road and continue on the path through the woodland, signposted 'to Crag Lane'. Pass a clearing with seats on your left and rejoin the tarmac footpath. There are some pleasant views on your right, the footpath leading down beside the wood to a road.

At the other side of the road are Harlow Car Gardens, the home of the Northern Horticultural Society. The entrance is fifty yards to your left. To continue to Birk Crag turn right when you reach the road. Pass a road on your left which leads down to the Harrogate Arms Hotel — refreshments can be taken in the hotel's garden in summer.

Continue straight along the lane which eventually swings right. Fork left as you approach the house onto a signposted path to Cornwall Road. You are now on top of Birk Crag, a large outcrop of rocks which tumble away to Oak Beck threading its way through Oakdale. There are some good views over the surrounding countryside.

The path descends through the rocks towards Oak Beck; some fifty yards above the river turn right along a broad path. It contours the hillside and leads to a gate onto Cornwall Road. Bear right up the road — there is a footpath on your left. Fork right at the main road junction and pass some toilets on your right.

The road re-enters the wood you passed through earlier. Forty yards into the wood, before your outgoing route, turn left along a broad woodland path. This leads round to the war memorial. Turn left down the tarmac path. At the point where the paths cross, carry straight on down the left side of Valley Gardens to the Pump Room Museum.

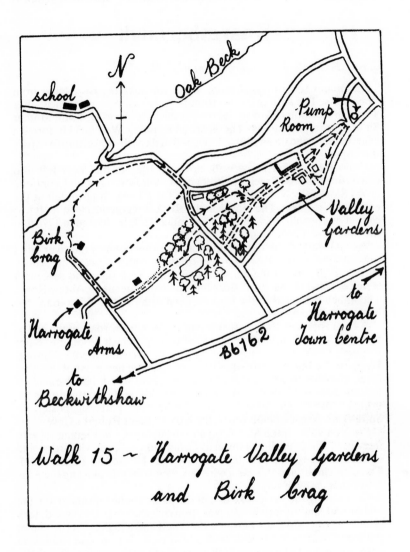

N

Oak Beck

school

Pump Room

Valley Gardens

Birk Crag

Harrogate Arms

B6162

to Harrogate Town Centre

to Beckwithshaw

Walk 15 ~ Harrogate Valley Gardens and Birk Crag

Walk 16   5½ miles (6 miles including Plumpton Rocks)

Knaresborough

Start: SE350569. Knaresborough Market Place.

THE quaint town of Knaresborough overlooks the river Nidd from steep cliffs. The ancient castle grounds, close to the Market Place, offer a superb viewpoint. Across the river is the cave associated with Mother Shipton, the prophetess. The nearby Dropping Well quickly forms a coat of limestone on anything deposited in its path, appearing to petrify the object.

From the Market Place walk down Castlegate and bear left into Cheapside. Cross Gracious Street into Windsor Lane and continue down Stockdale Walk. Turn right into Crag Lane and turn left at the end onto Crag Top. The House in the Rock is set on the cliffside. It was carved out of solid rock by a weaver called Hill; he started in 1770 and the task took him 16 years.

As you walk along Crag Top there are views across the river Nidd towards Plumpton. Pass two sets of steps which descend to Abbey Road. At the end of the houses on your left, fork right and descend a series of steps to the road. Bear left and continue along Abbey Road. The abbey belonged to the lesser known order of the Trinitarians but nothing now remains.

As you approach the Knaresborough to Wetherby road, at the end of a low stone wall on your right is a set of steps which descend to Saint Robert's Cave. In the cave Robert Flower lived the life of a hermit. When he died he was buried in the oblong grave hewn out of the solid rock; after his death oil flowed from his grave which had miraculous healing powers. Continue to the road junction and turn right over the bridge. Turn right again along the tarmac path signposted to Spitalcroft. You can look across the river to Saint Robert's Cave.

Walk past Plumpton Mill Farm and the caravan site keeping close to the river. The path climbs towards Grimbald Crag, set with trees, and offering a fine view across the river to Abbey House and a waterwheel. The path climbs and follows a wire fence on your left, skirting the edge of another caravan site.

On entering the wood take one of the paths up the hillside to join the higher path and turn right. As you approach the end of the wood, fork left on a delightful track between the wood and a hedge. At the end of the wood bear right around the field with a hedge on your right. The path curves left to Plumpton Hall Farm. Turn right as you approach the buildings then left.

To return to Knaresborough turn right just beyond the dutch barn along a stoned road. If you wish to see Plumpton Rocks, a beauty spot with eroded rocks, a lake and rhododendrons, continue up the access

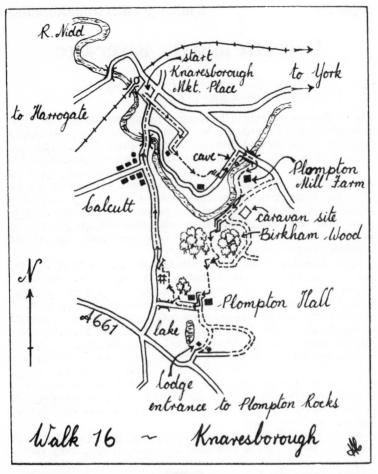

Walk 16 ~ Knaresborough

road from the farm. Curve right along the road to a lodge where a small fee is payable. Return to Plumpton Hall Farm and take the stoned lane beside the dutch barn.

Fork right through a gate before the bridge and follow the edge of the wood on your right. When it ends cross the field to a stile near the wood, bearing left around the field to a gate in a stone wall. Turn right along the road back to Knaresborough. Pass through Calcutt, cross the bridge near the Mother Shipton Inn and climb up Briggate. Turn left down Cheapside and Castlegate back into the Market Place.

There are plans, which are being opposed, to put a by pass through Birkham Wood.

Roecliffe and the River Ure

Start: A: SE395668. Road junction in Boroughbridge.
B: SE376659. Village green in Roecliffe.

FROM the road junction in the centre of Boroughbridge walk down the road southwards towards the A1. Turn right after fifty yards along a lane beyond the fish and chip shop; the lane curves left and right and leads to a T junction. Turn left along this lane to the Roecliffe road. On your right across the field are two of the Devil's Arrows — the third one stands beside the Roecliffe Road. Originally there were four stones, the other one being removed sometime in the 17th or 18th century. It is interesting to speculate how the local people erected these monoliths some 4,000 years ago; they each weigh between 30 and 36 tons. On reaching the road to Roecliffe, turn right, pass under the A1 and continue along the road into the village.

From the village green in Roecliffe take the path to the right of the church, signposted 'Public footpath to Westwick'. Pass through a kissing gate and cross the field to a stone stile built into the wall. Walk over the next field, bearing right, and descend to the river bank. A series of stiles and footbridges allow access along the public footpath beside the river bank. There were a large number of ducks and other bird life using the river and its banks as I walked this way.

After one and a half miles you approach a lock; to the right you can see a weir. The lock was part of the Ripon Canal which was constructed in 1773 to enable barges and other boats to reach Ripon. On your return you will turn off to the left here, through the white gate and along the access road. But first it is worth continuing along the river bank for half a mile to see Newby Hall.

As you approach the house you can see the park and walled gardens across the river. Then dramatically into view comes Newby Hall, a

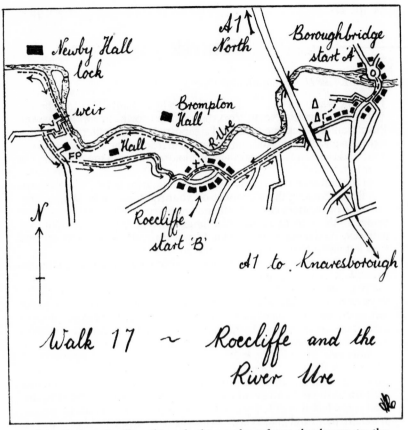

Walk 17 ~ Roecliffe and the River Ure

series of steps leading through the gardens from the house to the opposite river bank. The building dates from 1705 but it was greatly altered and improved by Robert Adam some seventy years later.

Return along the river bank to the lock. Turn right through the white gate and along the access road to join the road from Bishop Monkton to Roecliffe. Turn left along the road. After passing Hall Farm turn left through a gate, along the path signposted 'Public footpath to Roecliffe'. Cross the field to the left of the trough. Pass through a gate and follow the edge of the wood with a hedge on your right. A gate leads into a broad grassy lane. After passing Roecliffe Grange the tarmac road leads down to the road on the outskirts of Roecliffe. Turn left, then left again back to the village green.

For those walkers who started from Boroughbridge, continue along the road past the village green and then under the A1. Pass the Devil's Arrows and retrace your steps back into the centre of Boroughbridge.

Thirsk

Start: SE429821. Thirsk Market Place.

THIRSK was used as the basis of Darrowby in James Herriot's books and is still a typical North Yorkshire market town. From the Market Place walk up Kirkgate, the road signposted to Northallerton. On the right you pass Thirsk Museum. Turn left in front of the church and carry on round the bends, then straight on along a lane with the cemetery on your left.

At the end of the lane cross over a stile beside the gate. Cross the next two fields, keeping the wire fence on your right, to a stile. Walk along the edge of the field curving left and cross over a stile beside a sleeper bridge — this crosses a ditch. Continue with a hedge on your right to a gateway. At the end of the next field pass through a small gateway and turn left along the broad track at the edge of the field. After passing a plantation on your left, which appears to cover an interesting moated site, a farm lane leads down to the road.

Cross over the road, walk down the lane and fork right in 150 yards; the lane turns left around the edge of the wood. At the end of the wood turn left through a small gate, follow the edge of the field to another gate, then continue straight down the field with the hedge on your left. Turn right at the end of the field and pass through the cattle creep under the railway.

Carry straight on along the field, keeping the hedge on your left. Continue alongside three fields then turn left down a farm lane. Ignore the turn to the left and eventually the lane turns right and leads to the road. Turn left along the road. After three quarters of a mile turn right at a sharp bend and in ten yards turn left along a track along the edge of a field. In seventy yards turn right across the field to a small wooden bridge over a deep ditch.

Carry on along the edge of the field with trees on your right. Turn right near the end of the field and cross a sleeper bridge and stile, turning left between the wire fences to a stile. Turn right, then left, around the edge of the field to a road. Cross the next field to the railway line.

Cross carefully and quickly over the railway lines near the signal box. **Take care — the line is used by 125m.p.h. express trains.** Pass over the stile at the other side of the line near a red notice. Cross the field to a stile beside a wooden fence, walking down the next long field to pass straight into a lane with Thirsk church tower in front of you. Walk down the lane and turn right when you join the road. Take the first road on your left which brings you back to the church where you can turn right down Kirkgate to the Market Place.

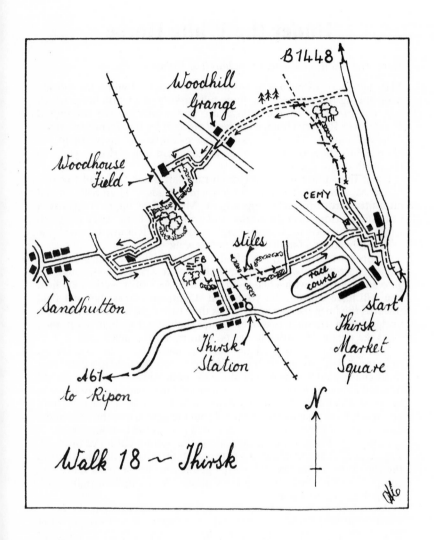

B1448

Woodhill Grange

Woodhouse Field

CEMY

stiles

FB

race course

Sandhutton

start

Thirsk Station

Thirsk Market Square

A61
to Ripon

N

Walk 18 ~ Thirsk

41

Walk 19   **4¾ miles or 5 miles**

Under the White Horse

Start: The small square near the church in Kilburn.

THE village of Kilburn is noted for two animals. High on the hillside
overlooking the village is the huge hill-carving of a white horse which
was cut in 1857. In the village are the workshops of the noted
woodcarver Robert Thompson; every piece of his oak furniture carries
a carved mouse. There are some fine examples of his work in the
church. His showrooms are in the Elizabethan house twenty yards to
the north of the square.

From the square near the church turn left down the road towards
Coxwold. Pass the road on your left which leads to High Kilburn and
after fifty yards turn right, opposite the Methodist Chapel. You cross a
little stone bridge over the stream and walk up the lane. After some 150
yards you can look back to your right and see the Kilburn White Horse
— it will become a familiar sight on this walk.

Ignore two turnings to the left and carry straight on. The lane bears
left and narrows between hedges, continuing to a gate. Pass through the
gate and continue with a hedge on your left. As you cross the next field
you will have a hedge on your right. Continue across the next field
towards the farm for some fifty yards then turn right down the field to a
bridge over a stream. Cross over the next field bearing slightly left, then
cross the next field, with a hedge on your right, to reach a road.

Turn right along the road and pass Common Hall. The road swings
right through a gateway; carry straight on across the field to a gate. Pass
through the gate and turn right along the hedgeside, cross a stream and
turn left along the hedgeside to join a broad farm road. Turn right along
the road which turns left after a short while. Continue on the road until
you reach High Osgoodby Grange. From the gate across the road at the
farm, turn back right across the field to a gate in the bottom corner.

Follow the hedge on your right along the bottom corner of the field.
Pass over a ditch and hedge at a gate and climb the next field to a gate in
the top corner. Continue with a hedge on your left, cross a fence and
continue to the road above Rose Cottage. You can turn right, back
along the road, to Kilburn.

Alternatively you can avoid the road but this alternative path may be
a little muddy at times. Turn left at the road above Rose Cottage. After
fifty yards turn right through a gate, then keep a wire fence on your left.
The route follows a valley with a small stream on your left which curves
to the right. Eventually cross over a bridge over the stream and follow
the farm lane which leads down to the outskirts of Kilburn. Turn right
back along the road into the village.

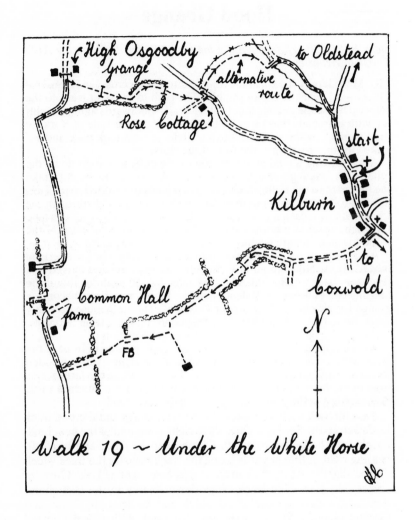

High Osgoodby Grange

to Oldstead

alternative route

Rose Cottage

start

Kilburn

to Coxwold

N

Common Hall Farm

FB

Walk 19 ~ Under the White Horse

Hood Grange

*Start: SE515830. The car park at the top of Sutton Bank on the A170
Thirsk to Helmsley road.*

FROM the large car park at the top of Sutton Bank cross the Helmsley–
Thirsk road near the top of the hill. The path to the right leads to the
cliff-top telescope and view indicator. Walk southwards along the cliff
top with extremely fine views on the right, across the Vale of York, to
the Pennines on the skyline. After a while you can look back and see
Lake Gormire nestling at the foot of the cliffs.

After walking a mile along the top of the cliffs fork right down the
railed path, passing a seat as you descend. At the foot of the cliffs take
the first path to the right which eventually leads to a stoned road. Turn
left and follow the winding road for a mile and a quarter, through the
trees, until you reach a T-junction. Turn right and in a quarter of a mile
turn right again at a bridleway sign. This leads along the edge of the
wood to a gate, a path leading across the field to Hood Grange.

An abbot and twelve monks from Furness Abbey in Cumberland
moved over to Hood about 1138; the site was small and they moved on a
few years later to Old Byland. They later moved again to found the
magnificent building at Byland Abbey. Hood may have become a
grange for Newburgh Priory near Coxwold. The farmhouse probably
dates from the 17th century but fragments of the earlier monastic
building have been incorporated during its construction.

As you approach the farm turn left at a gate, passing in front of the
farm with a wire fence on your right. Turn right over a wooden
footbridge and cross the field to a gate. Turn left along the farm access
road to the main road. Turn right along the road for a hundred yards
then turn left at the bridleway sign along the farm road.

Pass through a gate between the farm buildings and a broad track
leads across the field to a gate. Turn right at the end of the next field,
keeping the hedge on your left. Climb over the fence and turn left,
bearing right in fifteen yards along the track beneath the trees which
climbs slightly. At the fork in the tracks bear right as Lake Gormire
comes into view. The track drops down steeply to the lake shore.
Among the more unusual birds which may be seen are Green and
Greater Spotted Woodpecker and Nuthatch with Great Crested
Grebe and Coot on Lake Gormire.

Turn left along the path beside the lake. At the T-junction turn right.
After 150 yards a track turns steeply up the hillside, near a 'No fishing'
notice on a tree. In fifty yards you enter the Garbutt Wood Nature

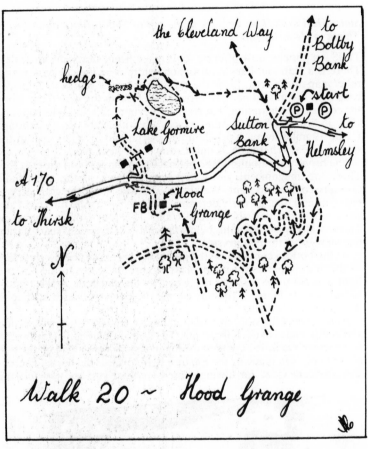

the Cleveland Way

to Boltby Bank

hedge

start

Lake Gormire

Sutton Bank

to Helmsley

A170

to Thirsk

Hood Grange

FB

N

Walk 20 ~ Hood Grange

Reserve and trail, forking right at the number 10 board. The well-used path climbs up to the top of the cliff. Here you turn right along the Cleveland Way long-distance footpath. A magnificent view opens out on your right of the cliffs of Roulston Scar and the outlying little peak of Hood Hill. The path leads back to Sutton Bank car park.

Sutton Bank and Kilburn White Horse

Start: SE515830. The car park at the top of Sutton Bank on the A170 Thirsk to Helmsley road.

THIS is a popular walk offering some magnificent views on a clear day. There is a National Park information centre near the car park with a relief map of the area. From the car park cross the Thirsk to Helmsley road near the milestone. The broad track follows the wire fence along the edge of the plantation. The track to the right leads to a telescope and view indicator. Among other places identified are Knaresborough Castle 19 miles away, York 20 miles, Richmond 24 miles and on the skyline Great Whernside 32 miles away in the Pennines.

The broad path alongside the plantation continues onto the crag top. There are magnificent views and looking back to the right Lake Gormire comes into sight. Walking southwards along the crag top you pass Casten Dike, an early defensive ditch. After a mile turn right at a signboard indicating the Forest Walk. The railed path, known as Thieves' Highway, descends below the cliffs, a convenient seat offering fine views over the countryside.

At the bottom continue on the path which bears left below the crags — the nesting places for many birds. Ignore the paths to the left and right and continue through the wood to the car park at the foot of Kilburn White Horse. Cross the car park to the steps which lead up to the gigantic hill carving.

At the foot of the steps two memorials give details of the construction and maintenance of the hill carving. The horse measures 314 feet by 228 feet and was cut in 1857. Climb the flight of steps which lead up the side of the horse. On reaching the top turn right towards the horse. There is a magnificent view, for having turned a corner you are now looking

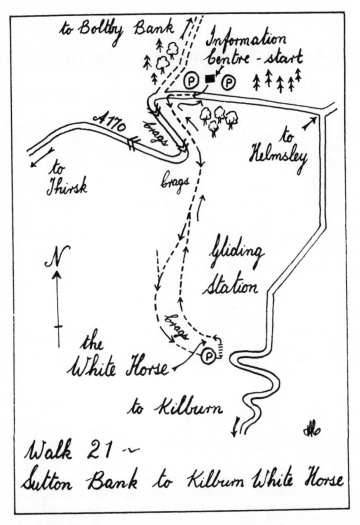

to Boltby Bank

Information
Centre - start

P ■ P

A170

crags

crags

to Thirsk

to Helmsley

N

Gliding
Station

crags

the
White Horse

P

crags

to Kilburn

Walk 21 ~
Sutton Bank to Kilburn White Horse

south towards York. On your left, in the valley, are the remains of
Byland Abbey and at the foot of the hill is the village of Kilburn, famous
for the workshops of Robert Thompson, the woodcarver.

Don't walk on the White Horse as this will only wear it away. The
patch of grass in the figure is its eye, although from close up it is hard to
identify. Continue along the cliff top with the glider station on your
right. Pass the track down Thieves' Highway you descended earlier and
retrace your steps back to Sutton Bank car park.

Lake Gormire and Hambleton Down

Start: SE515830. The car park at the top of Sutton Bank on the A170 Thirsk to Helmsley road.

AT the top of Sutton Bank are two large car parks and a National Park Information Centre. Part of this walk coincides with the Garbutt Wood Nature Trail and you may wish to obtain a leaflet from the centre. On the cliff top, just south of the road, is a view indicator and a telescope.

From the car park cross to the Cold Kirby road junction and take the broad track opposite, signposted public footpath. Bear right at the Cleveland Way sign in twenty yards. There is a magnificent prospect showing Lake Gormire at the foot of the cliffs and on over the patchwork of fields to Thirsk and beyond. Looking back you can see the crags of Roulston Scar and Hood Hill.

After a quarter of a mile, fork left past number 3 post on the nature trail. The path descends towards Lake Gormire, passing along the hillside and through the trees. From this area a soft sandstone was quarried for donkey stones, which were sold to housewives to leave a yellow edge to their newly cleaned steps.

You pass a large stone at post number 7 and at post 10 fork left on the path down to Lake Gormire. Turn right along the path on the lake shore, fork right after 200 yards and follow wooden catwalks across the muddy parts. At the T-junction, before Southwood Lodge, turn right uphill. The old hollow way has been worn out by the traffic which used it over many years.

The path climbs steeply — where it is muddy in the bottom the path has used the higher edges. Eventually you leave the wood and there is a small cliff in front of you. The path bears left along the edge of the wood and climbs the side of the cliff to join the Cleveland Way path. There is a magnificent view on your left with Thirlby and Boltby beneath you.

Turn right along the Cleveland Way for seventy yards. Near the end of the field on your left pass through a gate on your left. Walk along the edge of the field with a stone wall on your right. Pass a wood and you can either continue down the lane in front of you to Dialstone Farm and turn right along the road, or you can turn right at the end of the wood and cross Hambleton Down to the road on your left. Dialstone Farm was once an inn on the Hambleton Drove Road.

Horse racing took place on these downs as early as 1612. By 1714 it was the premier raceground of the North. The prizes included the Queen's Gold Cup valued at a hundred guineas. George I continued the tradition until 1720. This was a popular training area for the horses from Malton and horses are still trained here today. Turn right, down the road, to Sutton Bank car park.

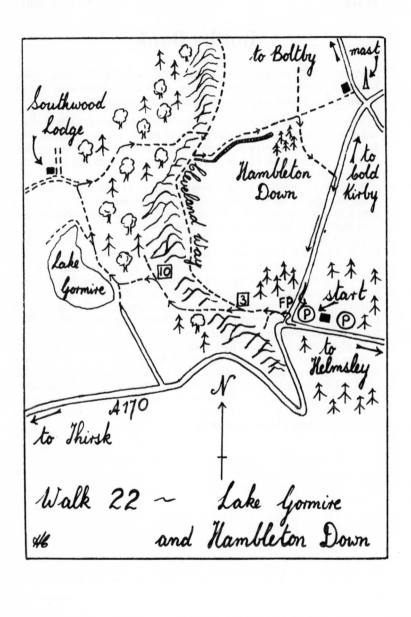

to Boltby

mast

Southwood Lodge

Hambleton Down

to bold Kirby

Cleveland Way

Lake Gormire

10

3

FP

start

P P

to Helmsley

A170

to Thirsk

N

Walk 22 ~ Lake Gormire and Hambleton Down

46

Boltby Bank

Start: SE509877. From the top of Sutton Bank take the Cold Kirby road,
bearing left after a mile towards Boltby. After a further two miles, at the
T-junction to Boltby and Hawnby, park in the lane ahead.

FROM the T-junction walk along the road signposted 'Cold Kirby 3
miles' for a mile. This road was formerly part of the old track used by
Scottish cattle drovers bringing animals south to be sold at the English
markets. By using this high-level route they avoided paying fees on the
toll roads to the west.

At the road junction to Old Byland turn right over a stile, walking
along the edge of the field with a wire fence on your left. Pass through a
gate and in thirty yards you are on a cliff top with a magnificent view
over Boltby and Felixkirk into the Vale of York.

Turn left on the Cleveland Way track along the cliff top for two
hundred yards to an iron age hill fort. On your approach you cross over
part of a defensive ditch. The fort stood on the edge of the cliff with fine
views of anything that happened below. In the field behind you is a
barrow which was once enclosed by the defensive ditch. After
inspecting the site, and the view, return back along the cliff top, passing
the gate you came through earlier. Continue along the Cleveland Way
path. Take care when crossing the top of the quarry.

The path continues past High Barn and across the middle of the field,
leaving the cliff top, to a gateway which leads onto a road. Cross over
the road, following the Cleveland Way markers, and continue on the
track which leads through the forestry to High Paradise Farm. Bear
right just beyond the farm buildings and walk up the lane to join the
Hambleton Drove Road. You can now turn right, down the broad lane,
back to the place where you started.

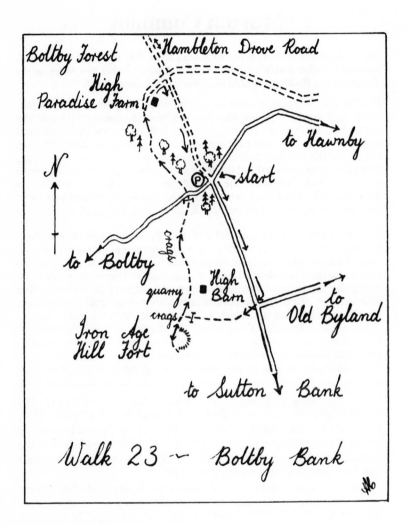

Boltby Forest

Hambleton Drove Road

High Paradise Farm

to Hawnby

N

start

to Boltby

crags

quarry

High Barn

crags

to Old Byland

Iron Age Hill Fort

to Sutton Bank

Walk 23 ~ Boltby Bank

Murton Common

*Start: SE509877. From the top of Sutton Bank take the Cold Kirby road,
bearing left after a mile towards Boltby. After a further two miles, at the
T-junction to Boltby and Hawnby, park in the lane ahead.*

FROM the T-junction walk along the road signposted to Hawnby.
After half a mile turn left through the second gateway opposite the
barn. You have a stone wall on your left which sweeps right and
continues as a wire and pole fence. At the end of the field the path
sweeps to the left and continues with a stone wall on your right. Pass
through a gate at the end of the field and continue along a distinct path
across the field. Bear left in the dip and eventually follow a stone wall on
your right. The track sweeps left and descends to a gate in a small valley;
continue along the track which leads across the field to join an
unsurfaced road.

In front of you is the wooded valley of Thorodale with North Moor
Wood. At the foot of this valley was the Benedictine nunnery at Arden
Hall. Turn left along the unsurfaced road for 1½ miles to a gate where
you reach the Hambleton Drove Road. You will be turning left back
along the drove road but first admire the scenery in this wild and
desolate part of the North York Moors. Beyond the wall is a fine view
over Kepwick Moor and Nether Silton to the Vale of York. To the
right, about a hundred yards along the drove road, are the ruins of
Limekiln House, a wayside inn used by the drovers. The stone-walled
fields can also be seen where the cattle could be kept overnight.

Turning southwards on the drove road you follow the wall on your
right. You eventually pass two stones beside the track inscribed "C.T.
1770" indicating an estate boundary and when it was surveyed. The
Scottish drovers were a skilled and trusted breed of men. They
gathered the cattle together and drove them along the tracks south to
the markets, arriving in time to put back some of the weight lost on the
journey. Having sold them they would return north to pay the people
who had entrusted them with their cattle.

The drove road leaves the moor and enters Boltby Forest at Steeple
Cross. The original wayside cross has gone but a rough stone shaft
also inscribed "C.T. 1770" stands to the east of the gate. Continue on
the broad track through the forest to another gate then continue along
the broad walled lane, its width is a good indication of a drove road
used for the passage of many cattle. After a mile you return to the top
of Boltby Bank where you started.

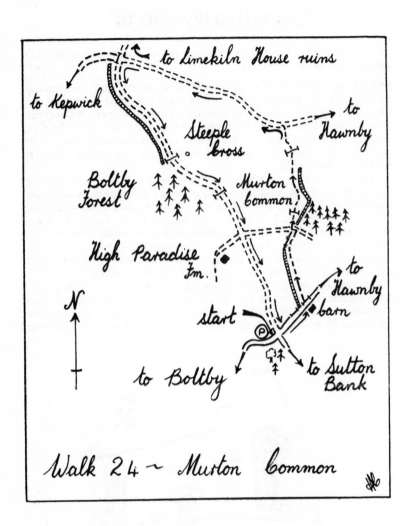

to Limekiln House ruins

to Kepwick

to Hawnby

Steeple cross

Boltby Forest

Murton Common

High Paradise Fm.

N

to Hawnby

barn

start

to Boltby

to Sutton Bank

Walk 24 ~ Murton Common

Osmotherley Circuit

Start: SE456973. Osmotherley village centre. One mile east of the A19 Thirsk to Middlesbrough road.

FROM the centre of Osmotherley walk up North End, the road to Swainby. On the outskirts of the village turn left along Ruebury Lane where there is a Cleveland Way signpost. A fine view opens out over the plain below. There is an indicator where the road forks. The right fork leads to The Lady Chapel, a curious little church attached to a house. It was built by Queen Catherine of Aragon for the recluse Thomas Parkinson about 1515.

From the fork in the track near the indicator bear left. Walk past Chapel Wood Farm, pass through a gate with a waymarker and carry on with the hedge on your left. A gate leads through into a wood where you fork right along a path signposted 'Cleveland Way'. The path climbs steadily beneath the trees. On reaching the top follow the stone wall on your right. Continue through the gate passing the post office relay station. After a hundred yards you can see a triangulation pillar on your right — this was the original start of the Lyke Wake Walk.

Pass through two gates and follow the broad track across the moor, ignoring the track to the left. The path eventually descends along a wallside into Scarth Nick; there are fine views to the north east over the Cleveland Plain. On reaching the road turn right. When the road turns

Lady Chapel ~ Osmotherley

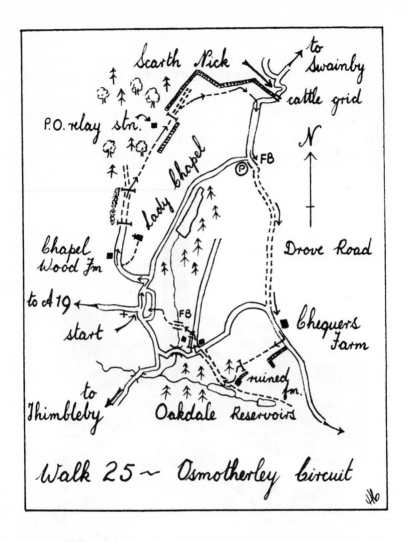

Walk 25 ~ Osmotherley Circuit

left, near the car park, carry straight on over a white footbridge. The broad path sweeps up the hillside. This rough track was used by Scottish drovers bringing their cattle south to the markets.

After a mile and a quarter this road joins the Osmotherley–Hawnby road. Bear left down to Chequers Farm, once an inn — you may still be able to get some refreshments. Fifty yards beyond Chequers Farm turn right along a signposted path, following a stone wall on your left. At the corner carry straight on along the track across the open moor. Pass through a gate and continue descending into Oakdale with a wall on your left.

Turn right near the ruined building, pass through a gate and over a bridge. A lane climbs through a wood and passes along the edge of two fields to the road. Turn left, then in 25 yards turn right at a Cleveland Way sign. Walk up the lane for 150 yards then turn left through a stile beyond the gate to White House. Turn right before the farm buildings and a path descends across the field to a footbridge over the stream. Steps lead up through the wood; cross over the field towards Osmotherley church tower. Cross over the Back Lane and a cobbled path leads back into the centre of Osmotherley.